A ROOKIE READER

SNOW JOE

By Carol Greene

Illustrations by Paul Sharp

Prepared under the direction of Robert Hillerich, Ph.D.

CHILDRENS PRESS ™

CHICAGO

This book is for Joe!

Library of Congress Cataloging in Publication Data

Greene, Carol.
  Snow Joe.

  (A Rookie reader)
  Summary: Throw. Blow. Whoa! Joe does many
things with snow.
  [1. Snow—Fiction. 2. Stories in rhyme]
I. Sharp, Paul (Paul W.), ill. II. Title.
III. Series.
PZ8.3.G82Sn 1982   [E]   82-9403
ISBN 0-516-02035-8   AACR2

Joe! Joe!

3

Snow, Joe!

Snow!

Go, Joe.

Go. Go!

Blow, snow.

Blow at Joe.

Throw, Joe.

Throw that snow.

Roll, Joe.

Roll in snow.

Oh, Joe!

Go, go!

Whoa, Joe!

Whoa . . . oh!

Ho ho!

Ho ho!

Roll, Joe.

Roll that snow.

Grow, snow.

Grow, grow . . .

Oh, Joe!

Show, show!

Slow, Joe.

Go slow.

Slow Joe.

Blow, Joe.

Oh, JOE!

WORD LIST

at	in	slow
blow	Joe	snow
go	oh	that
grow	roll	throw
ho	show	whoa

About the Author

Carol Greene has written over 20 books for children, plus stories, poems, songs, and filmstrips. She has also worked as a children's editor and a teacher of writing for children. She received a B.A. in English Literature from Park College, Parkville, Missouri, and an M.A. in Musicology from Indiana University. Ms. Greene lives in St. Louis, Missouri. When she isn't writing, she likes to read, travel, sing, do volunteer work at her church — and write some more. Her *The Super Snoops and the Missing Sleepers* and *Sandra Day O'Connor, First Woman on the Supreme Court* have also been published by Childrens Press.

About the Artist

Paul Sharp graduated from the Art Institute of Pittsburgh.
He has worked for the Curtis Publishing Company as Art Director of Child Life magazine.
At the present time he works as a free-lance artist at his home in Indianapolis, Indiana.